# Can You Tell a Gecko from a Salamander?

## Buffy Silverman

Lerner Publications Company
Minneapolis

To the Viceroy, long may you reign!

Lerner Publications Company
A division of Lerner Publishing Group, Inc.
241 First Avenue North
Minneapolis, MN 55401 U.S.A.

Website address: www.lernerbooks.com


Library of Congress Cataloging-in-Publication Data

Silverman, Buffy.
    Can you tell a gecko from a salamander? / by Buffy Silverman.
        p. cm.   —  (Lightning bolt books.™ — Animal look-alikes)
    Includes index.
    ISBN 978-0-7613-6737-6 (lib. bdg. : alk. paper)
        1. Geckos—Juvenile literature. 2.  Salamanders—
Juvenile literature.  I. Title.
QL666.L245S55  2012
597.8'5—dc23                                        2011022539

Manufactured in the United States of America
1 — PP — 12/31/11

# Table of Contents

# Scaly or Smooth

This animal is called a day gecko.

Geckos and salamanders look a lot alike. Long tails stretch from their thin bodies. They walk on four short legs.

They hunt insects, spiders, and worms. Their teeth grip their prey. Then they swallow.

This worm became prey for a salamander. Prey are animals that another animal hunts and eats.

But you can tell them apart.
Geckos are reptiles. Reptiles
have dry skin. Their skin is
covered with hard plates
called scales.

This gecko has scaly skin.

Salamanders are amphibians. Most amphibians have moist skin. Their skin does not have scales.

This salamander has smooth skin, like most frogs. Frogs are also amphibians.

Scales help hold water inside a gecko's body. They keep it from drying out. So geckos can live far from water. This Namib web-footed gecko lives in the desert.

Salamanders stay in damp places. They crawl through leaves or dig below ground. They swim in streams.

A spring salamander waves its body to swim in a stream.

Salamanders breathe through their skin. They need moist skin to breathe. Many salamanders also breathe with lungs or gills.

Mudpuppies are a kind of salamander. They wriggle their gills to breathe underwater.

Geckos cannot breathe through skin. Their lungs breathe air. Air enters and leaves through a gecko's nose.

This leopard gecko breathes through its nose.

# Egg Time

Rain falls on a spring night. A slender salamander crawls through the woods. She stops at a pond. Hundreds of salamanders have gathered to lay eggs.

The salamander swims underwater. She lays a big clump of eggs and swims away. The eggs have no shells. A clear jelly covers them. Turtles, frogs, and insects eat most of the eggs.

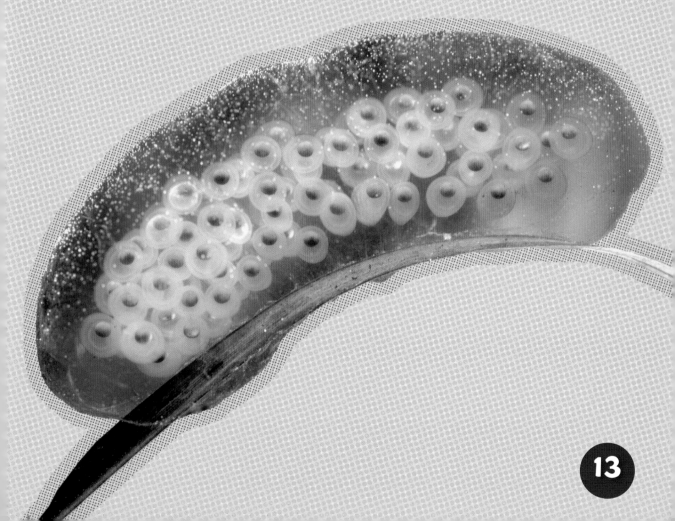

Geckos lay their eggs on land. A leaf-tailed gecko lays two eggs. She hides them under leaves. Then the mother gecko crawls away. Shells protect the eggs.

A tokay gecko sticks her eggs to a rock. The soft shells harden in the dry air. The parents guard the eggs until they hatch. The parents keep away predators. Predators are animals that hunt and eat other animals.

These tokay geckos protect their eggs. Red-backed salamanders also guard their eggs.

# Growing Up

Most young salamanders hatch from eggs in a pond or a stream. They live in water and breathe with gills.

These young spotted salamanders grow in a pond.

Geckos hatch from eggs that are on land. How does a baby crack its shell? It uses a special tooth called an egg tooth.

Most baby salamanders look very different from their parents. The young have tail fins. These help them dart through the water. They hunt water insects and tadpoles. They grow quickly.

A young gecko looks like a tiny adult. This fan-footed gecko sneaks up on spiders and insects. Then it grabs them. It hunts and eats all night. When the sun rises, it hides in a cave or in a crack in a large rock.

The colors of this fan-footed gecko help it blend in with rocks.

Many salamanders change shape as they grow. Their tail fin disappears. They lose their gills and grow lungs. They also shed their skin. They leave the water to live on land.

This young blue-spotted salamander will change as it grows into an adult (bottom).

As a gecko grows, its skin gets too tight.  It pulls its old skin off with its sharp teeth.  It eats the old skin that it sheds.

# Keeping Safe

A hungry bird lands near a gecko. The gecko turns so its fat tail faces the bird. The bird reaches for the gecko. Suddenly the gecko's tail comes off!

This gecko is just starting to grow a new tail.

The bird pecks the wiggling tail. It does not see the gecko escape. In a few weeks, the gecko grows a new tail.

Salamanders can take off their tails too.  A dusky salamander's tail jerks and wiggles.  A garter snake eats the tail, but the salamander escapes.

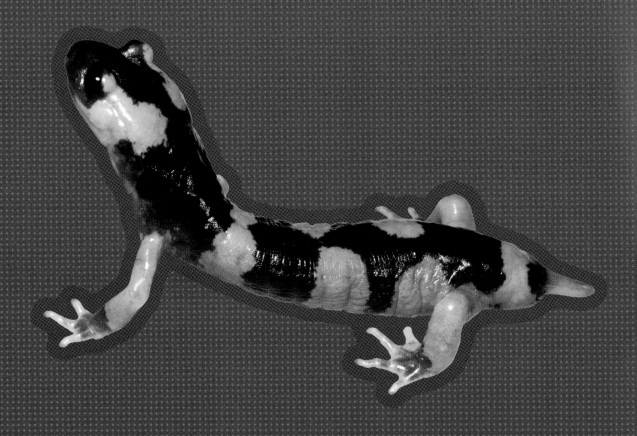

It grows a new tail.

Salamanders also have special glands in their skin. The glands make bad-tasting liquids or poisons. They can make a predator sick.

A salamander's bright color warns about its poisons. Birds leave this red eft alone.

Most geckos hide from predators. But a tokay gecko attacks when it feels danger. It blows up its body and hisses. It opens its jaw. Then it rushes at the animal and bites. It does not let go.

Geckos skitter across rocks and sand. They climb trees and walls. Salamanders swim in ponds and streams. They creep under leaves.

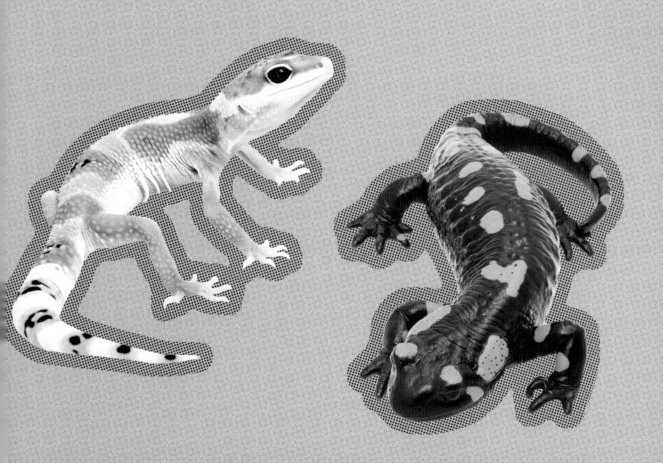

Can you tell these look-alikes apart?

# Who Am I?

Look at the pictures below. Which ones are geckos? Which ones are salamanders?

 I have dry, scaly skin.

I keep my smooth skin moist.

 A clear jelly covers my eggs.

Shells cover my eggs.

 When I am young, I crawl on land.

When I am young, I swim in water.

Answers:
column 1: gecko, salamander, gecko; column 2: salamander, gecko, salamander

# Fun Facts

- Imagine climbing up a wall and across the ceiling. A gecko can do that! Millions of tiny hairs cover the bottom of a gecko's feet. Each hair splits into many smaller hairs. The hairs cling to almost any surface.

- Geckos squeak, click, croak, and bark. Their sounds help them find one another. They also tell other geckos to stay away.

- Salamanders are silent. They cannot hear sounds. But they feel the ground shake. That tells them when others are near.

- A Japanese giant salamander lives up to its name. It can grow to the length of a person. Male giant salamanders guard the nest where eggs are laid.

# Glossary

**amphibian:** an animal with smooth skin that usually lives part of its life on land. Salamanders are amphibians.

**gills:** a body part that some animals use to breathe underwater

**gland:** a body part that makes and releases chemicals

**insect:** an animal that has six legs and three main body parts as an adult

**lungs:** a body part that some animals use to breathe air

**predator:** an animal that hunts and eats other animals

**prey:** an animal that is hunted and eaten by other animals

**reptile:** an animal with scaly skin and a backbone. Reptiles breathe air. Geckos are reptiles.

**scale:** a hard plate that covers and protects a reptile's skin

**skitter:** to move quickly and lightly

# Further Reading

Bishop, Nic. *Nic Bishop Lizards.* New York: Scholastic Nonfiction, 2010.

Fleisher, Paul. *Desert Food Webs.* Minneapolis: Lerner Publications Company, 2008.

Lamstein, Sarah Marwil. *Big Night for Salamanders.* Honesdale, PA: Boyds Mills Press, 2010.

National Geographic Kids Creature Features: Gecko
http://kids.nationalgeographic.com/kids/animals/creaturefeature/geckos

National Geographic Kids Creature Features: Spotted Salamander
http://kids.nationalgeographic.com/kids/animals/creaturefeature/salamander

Photo Safari: Gecko
http://www.nationalgeographic.com/ngextremeexplorer/1009/photo_safari.html

# Index

# Photo Acknowledgments

The images in this book are used with the permission of: © Joel Sartore/National Geographic/Getty Images, pp. 1 (top), 22; © Geoff Brightling/Dorling Kindersley/Getty Images, p. 1 (bottom); © m3 m3/Imagebroker.net/Photolibrary, p. 2; © Peter Weber/Photographer's Choice/Getty Images, p. 4; © NHPA/SuperStock, p. 5; © Cathy Keifer/Shutterstock Images, pp. 6, 11, 28 (top left); © Ryan M. Bolton/Shutterstock Images, pp. 7, 28 (top right); © Solvin Zankl/Visuals Unlimited, Inc., p. 8; © Nature's Images, Inc./Photo Researchers, Inc., p. 9; © National Geographic/SuperStock, p. 10; © Robin Loznak/ZUMA Press/Corbis, p. 12; © Dwight R. Kuhn, pp. 13, 16, 23, 25, 28 (middle left); © Steimer/ARCO/naturepl.com, pp. 14, 28 (middle right); © Cliff Flock, p. 15; © Animals Animals/SuperStock, pp. 17, 19, 21, 28 (bottom left); © Gary Meszaros/Photo Researchers, Inc., pp. 18, 28 (bottom right); © Michael Redmer/Visuals Unlimited, Inc., p. 20 (top); © James Deboer/Dreamstime.com, p. 20 (bottom); © Joseph T. Collins/Photo Researchers, Inc., p. 24; © Lacz, Gerard/Animals Animals, p. 26; © iStockphoto.com/Rhett Olson, p. 27 (left); © iStockphoto.com/Cristian Mihai Vela, p. 27 (right); © iStockphoto.com/Brian Snyder, p. 30; © George Grall/National Geographic/Getty Images, p. 31.

Front cover: © Apostrophe Productions/Getty Images (top); © James Deboer/Dreamstime.com (bottom).

Main body text set in Johann Light 30/36.